FIND DESIGNING LOCAL ONLINE

WWW.DESIGNINGLOCAL.COM

HI@DESIGNINGLOCAL.COM

DESIGNINGLOCAL

FACEBOOK.COM/DESIGNINGLOCALPLACES

LINKEDIN.COM/IN/KYLEEZELL

SOUNDCLOUD.COM/DESIGNINGLOCAL

@DESIGNINGLOCAL

DESIGNINGLOCAL.TUMBLR.COM

PINTEREST.COM/KYLEEZELL/PINS

VIMEO.COM/DESIGNINGLOCAL

SNAIL-MAIL

KYLE EZELL
THE OHIO STATE UNIVERSITY
KNOWLTON SCHOOL
COLUMBUS, OHIO 43210 USA

PRAISE

"Progressive-minded planners have a whole toolkit of best practices that they use to ensure that their communities put their best faces forward, but the problem with best practices is that they become templates. Transform enough abandoned mills into cute artisanal-gastro-boutiques, repurpose enough suburban strip malls into the same mixed-use live-play-shop destinations, and you are simply replacing one form of generica with another.

Kyle Ezell has written an important and timely manifesto that challenges planners, designers, and place-makers of every stripe to stop confusing imitation with innovation. There are 90,000 municipalities in the US and every one of them has its own story to tell. As *Designing Local* makes abundantly clear, local integrity is more than an esthetic preference. Authentic design is a powerful driver of economic development."

RICHARD FLORIDA
UNIVERSITY OF TORONTO, NYU, THE ATLANTIC CITIES
AUTHOR OF THE RISE OF THE CREATIVE CLASS

"While every company tries to convince you of how much different and better it is than every other company, every city tries its hardest to convince you it's exactly like every other city that's conventionally considered cool. In *Designing Local*, Kyle Ezell tackles this head on, calling on cities to avoid merely chasing fads and to think hard about their own unique character while recognizing the role that best practices can play. It's a needed corrective to the lemming-like behavior of all too many of our communities."

AARON RENN
PUBLISHER OF THE URBANOPHILE, WWW.URBANOPHILE.COM

"What richness has been lost by our temporary neglect of 'The Local!' We are all sick to death of mass production and consumption and the soul-numbing cities - if you can even call them that - that result. This book provides the intellectual weight to synergize 'The Local' movement, helping it catapult out of the sidelines and into the spotlight.

We now have the necessary ingredients to fully propagate Jane Jacobs' complex urbanism: an appreciation of finely-grained urbanity, a focus on sustainability, and a public fed up with a corporate-first, top-down aesthetic that created the urban mess we have been forced to endure. *Designing Local* leverages the design sensibility of an inchoate but energized movement, helping to devise synergistic strategies that will make local sensibility become the modus operandi of cities throughout the U.S. and beyond."

EMILY TALEN, FAICP
ARIZONA STATE UNIVERSITY AND AUTHOR OF CITY RULES

"Today's forward-looking communities compete globally for people and investment, often by modeling each other's strategies. Unfortunately, that's not always a clear path to success. Kyle Ezell deftly turns the standard global approach on its ear by showing how nourishing 'The Local' can be the best way to stand out from the rest. To be clear, this isn't a 'Main Street' community planning approach; it's a 'Your Street' community excellence strategy. Community leaders will find *Designing Local* both a straightforward call to action and an enjoyable read. By building on unique traits, communities can provide an intoxicating choice for newcomers and visitors while reinforcing a proud local identity."

WILLIAM MURDOCK, AICP
EXECUTIVE DIRECTOR, MID-OHIO REGIONAL PLANNING COMMISSION

DESIGNING LOCAL

REVEALING OUR TRUEST COMMUNITIES

Kyle Ezell

Designing Local
Revealing Our Truest Communities

By Kyle Ezell

Cover design by Jon Myers (jonmyers.com)
Book design and layout by Zachary E. Kenitzer

Printed in the United States of America

First Edition, July 2014

ISBN-10: 069223330X
ISBN-13: 978-0-692-23330-6

Published by The Look Up Project, Ltd.

www.DesigningLocal.com

ACKNOWLEDGEMENTS

Thanks to Bob Mick, Phil Arnold, Gary Mann, Rich Bailey, and Ann Coulter (of Chattanooga) for your ears during these years of writing this book. Love to my professor colleagues in Ohio State's City and Regional Planning Program for your support and encouragement. Thanks also to Zach Kenitzer, Josh Lapp, and Amanda Golden for your help in editing and ideas for this abbreviated (and admittedly risky) "Let's lure blog readers to this book" design. My sincerest appreciation to my academic mentor, Fritz Gritzner, who taught me to think this way. Finally, my deepest appreciation to my father and mother, Ray and Glenda Ezell; sisters Mindy Riley and Emily Stacey; and my extended family for putting up with me as an urban planning geek for most of my life.

Ralph Waldo Emerson said, "People wish to be settled; only as far as they are unsettled is there any hope for them."

My hope with this book is to unsettle the fields of city planning and design.

Designing Local is meant to be read and
absorbed at once so you can
take action immediately

Please pass it around and talk about it so
others might also take action.

CONTENTS

A NEW WAY

I'm going to tweak your thinking about city planning and urban design.

My goal is to inspire you to make your community shine.

Transforming the place you love into a truly unique place will increase its economic competitiveness.

But this book has few new ideas.

This book isn't about ideas, especially specific ideas that are sure to work for your local community. You shouldn't expect any step-by-step instructions or quick-fix formulas in the following pages. Most of all, I certainly will not provide a showcase of best practices that provide solutions to the problems that cities face, something virtually every other book on this subject offers. Instead, I'm offering a new way of looking at planning and design to help professionals and everyday citizens become inspired to create cities from the inside out, while recognizing the forces that hinder ingenuity and success. It's a call for people who care to choose to become empowered and emboldened, so they can help make transformative physical expressions happen in their local communities.

As a planning and design philosophy book with a definitive point of view, the ideas herein are hardly new. Vast resources have long been available for learning methods for improving the appearance and character of places. Yet the problem persists:

despite the many, varied contributions to urban planning and design published over the years, too many of our cities and towns still seem uninspired.

OUR INFORMATION CRISIS

I believe that it is important for me to thank the folks who have been working and thinking hard on bettering places. Even though I appreciate their contributions, I am convinced that existing planning and design literature isn't translating effectively into practice, and it certainly isn't providing the inspiration needed to be creative or to create remarkable places. As a result, I believe that places are bearing the brunt of an information crisis. We must face this crisis head on.

STUCK MINDSETS

It seems to me that the conversations in planning and design are often derived from the same books whether they are new, popular publications or classics that we all return to. When we huddle in our professional reading groups, conversations end up feeling like an abstract recital of a book report in a classroom. With so many methods, philosophies, and formulas available to us, we devolve into inattentive students who either aren't listening or don't believe that real change can happen. I notice this at professional conferences where it's even worse: we stand around and talk, talk, and talk some more. We listen to "best practice" seminars where the same concepts—ones that are almost always in these books—are beat into our heads, and then we sit through more seminars featuring examples of cities and towns that are implementing those "original" ideas in a seemingly endless iterative way. These are portrayed as the smart evolution of next-generation ideas or as masterpieces of urban design. Instead, what we end up doing is designing caricatures of a caricature. Our places are no longer genuine, and we have lost sight of why.

GREAT BOOKS AREN'T WORKING

If you're in the profession, you'd have to agree that we've generally become numb to ingenuity; we seem to favor the well-worn paths of plans past. Since we're all thinking and doing the same things, it's no wonder that the good books on community character haven't made our communities stand out.

For example, one of the most important books that my academic colleagues are quick to point to as a "game changer" book in planning for character and aesthetics is *Design With Nature* by Ian McHarg, first published back in 1967. It's a masterful book that focuses on the idea that real estate developments should be influenced by the original surrounding natural state, and manmade environments should point to a particular community's ecology. It's a simple and important idea for planners and urban designers, which is why the book received tremendous reviews such as this prominent one from the back cover of a 25-year anniversary reprint:

*In the twenty-five years since it first took the academic world by storm, **Design With Nature** has done much to redefine the fields of landscape architecture, urban and regional planning, and ecological design. It has also left a permanent mark on the ongoing discussion of mankind's place in nature and nature's place in mankind within the physical sciences and humanities. Described by one enthusiastic reviewer as a "user's manual for our world," **Design With Nature** offers a practical blueprint for a new, healthier relationship between the built environment and nature. In so doing, it provides nothing less than the scientific, technical, and philosophical foundations for a mature civilization that will, as Lewis Mumford ecstatically put it in his Introduction to the 1969 edition, "replace the polluted, bulldozed, machine-dominated, dehumanized, explosion threatened world that is even now disintegrating and disappearing before our eyes."*

After the publishing of *Design With Nature* and in the decades that followed, planners and urban designers everywhere were supposedly inspired and implementing these ideas into plans throughout the United States and the world. According to professionals I know who practiced planning and urban design during this time, the book ushered in a new ecological design movement, which spurred a greater focus on analysis-driven processes to evaluate local ecologies and physical contexts as a framework for shaping human habitat. But how widespread was the influence of the book, and what impact did it actually have on our communities?

I argue that an ample amount of time has passed—several real estate development cycles—to allow a proper assessment of the book's real impact. Outside of some high-profile mega-subdivisions such as McHarg's famous "The Woodlands," a mostly residential development north of Houston, Texas, which respects the forest the homes are nestled in, and the naturalized built environment associated with parts of Amelia Island, Florida, a beach community, where are the rest of these ecology-based communities?

Mumford, an original reviewer, could not have been more wrong about the future he was seeing because, on a large scale, we have absolutely not replaced the "polluted, bulldozed, machine-dominated, dehumanized, explosion-threatened world." Less-than-ideal, thoughtless development has not disintegrated and disappeared before our eyes. In fact, unfortunate, ecologically-void landscapes have only proliferated during the past 50 years of what was supposed to be a revolution. There was no game change!

READ. THINK. IGNORE.

I believe that if McHarg were alive today, he would be disappointed by all the communities that decided not to respect their natural environments; just think about the egregious examples of golf course communities in Phoenix and Las Vegas. Their green, manicured grass doesn't fit in at all with the indigenous red, dusty natural environments they're surrounded by, but irrigated golf courses still dot the landscape in both of these cities' metropolitan areas. In the Midwest, man-made mounds I refer to as sod-dunes, which resemble beach sand dunes, have proliferated in suburban towns. These six-foot high compacted, fabricated earth mounds follow the street contours to shield commercial and residential development from the drivers' view, and the driver's view of the backside of commercial and residential development. Thousands of miles of such untold scenes snake through former farms and prairies, in open defiance of the flat terrain geography that characterizes the Midwest.

I have talked to many architects who have been inspired by nature to design individual homes and other structures with ties to the environment, and I have seen good work in communities that were probably somehow influenced by *Design With Nature*, but there is clear evidence that a vast number of places generally ignore their local ecology unless they are forced to do so by some environmental law with teeth, rather than because of McHarg's design evangelism.

My interest in this topic originated in 1992 when I read James Howard Kunstler's *The Geography of Nowhere: The Rise and Decline of America's Man-Made Landscape* while studying geography in graduate school. This brilliant book pointed out, in a simple and entertaining way, how cities in the U.S. had evolved from interesting places to "dead zones" and how the rural and suburban areas had become "a wasteland of cartoon architecture and parking lots." This book was a personal and professional game-changer for me. Previously, I hadn't thought much about our communities and the mess we'd made of them. When you're born into a community, or grow up in it, you're far less likely to question and critique it. Regardless of my personal attachment to this book, it was certainly not a game changer in the practice of planning and design. Nearly 25 years later, we're still reciting book reports about the vast homogeneity of our communities. As we drone on in conferences, meetings, and offices our places are becoming even more "nowhere" than ever, making them even less special and appealing.

More recently I've enjoyed *The Economics of Uniqueness* published by the World Bank (2011). It is a fresh addition to planning and design because it provides a fairly comprehensive focus on the regeneration of downtowns, historic neighborhoods, adaptive reuse of buildings, and the strong relationship between unique places and economic development. This publication even suggests that communities that decide to protect their character and encourage new development that celebrates cultural heritage are more likely to reduce poverty, bring jobs, and increase the quality of life. It's an exciting read for planners like me. However, as a test of the effectiveness and reach of this publication three years after its release date, I conducted a quick poll of 20 colleagues of mine who work in the trenches. I asked them if they had ever heard of *The Economics of Uniqueness* and if they knew that it was free to download from the World Bank's website. Not one of them did. Most shrugged, and it's the shrug that concerns me most.

If this piece of work, published by a major international institution, has not impacted professionals, then how will my own book change the state of urban planning?

So many good books and scholarly articles touch on the importance of designing unique cities and towns, even offering practical suggestions and case studies. I feel a need to showcase these excellent works here, many of which I've been influenced by although I am reminded that I am not writing a dissertation where a vast bibliography would be required or desired. However, I do want to mention geographer Yi-Fu Tuan's *Topophilia: A Study of Environmental Perception, Attitudes, and Values* (1973), a thoughtful study of the bond between people's values, perceptions, and relationships to place. Additionally, Tony Hiss' *The Experience of Place: A New Way of Looking at and Dealing With our Radically Changing Cities and Countryside* (1991) asks some excellent questions. For example, he asks, "Why do some places—the concourse of Grand Central Terminal or a small farm or even the corner of a skyscraper—affect us so mysteriously and yet so forcefully?" Hiss asks the bigger questions that are critical to a planner's educational process (and are fun to think about, too). I greatly appreciate Emily Talen's work, especially *City Rules: How Regulations Affect Urban Form* (2011), a book about how community leaders can understand how rules work, how they affect the landscape, and which rules could have prevented bad things from happening. I'd also be remiss if I didn't acknowledge the powerful classic, *The Image of the City* by Kevin Lynch (1961), a scholarly book that explores the meaning of a city's form to the people who live there.

Let me also mention Randal Arendt's *Rural by Design: Maintaining Small Town Character* (1994), a book that I consider to have made some important contributions to the field of urban planning. He introduced conservation design—dense houses in a tight village format instead of conventional subdivisions with scant open space. Ellen Dunham-Jones' *Retrofitting Suburbia; Urban Design Solutions for Redesigning Suburbs* (2009) made some waves with her call to make suburban communities more dense and walkable, and some suburbs are making changes; but considering the vast literature in city planning and design, practitioners end up having to pick and choose between the various experts. There are so many voices that want to be heard. What often ends up happening is that the loudest voices win in a kind of high school popularity contest. For instance, for a long time, rural subdivisions in the Arendt style were in style for some country villages that bought into his ideas.

While I am a fan of some of these projects because some do provide needed opportunities for citizens and business alike, I do not believe that planning and designing communities should be treated as a robotic, "one-size-fits-all" professional exercise. Urban design will never be, and should not be, a hard science.

BEST PRACTICES RUT

The same is true for organizations that do work in planning and design. They advocate for creating special places, but they are designing places based upon the experiences of other places. Places that are doing the same things can't possibly be remarkable. While reviewing best practices is useful (as it allows professionals to chart the seas of knowledge) we have strayed too far in viewing best practices as being implementable anywhere. We have made them a commodity; the implementation of best practices has become the planner and designer's widget. This is why, from this point on, there are no local place-based examples in this book—and any and all places that are referenced are generalized to point out universal issues.

WHY MY PROFESSIONAL WORK IS NOT FEATURED

While I've been strongly advised to provide actual examples of things I've succeeded in implementing so others can adopt my methodology to their places, I believe that doing so would be a contradiction. This book will not become yet another collection of case studies in "good design." It refuses to look at places with best practices, places with worst practices, or places that have original perspectives. (The latter may not currently exist.)

The moment a practice is accepted and implemented "to spec" is another bad moment for the urban design professions that have chosen to stamp out yet another unremarkable place. That moment is an open rejection of creativity. Adopting a practice from somewhere else, without thinking about context and local appropriateness, is lazy, and laziness is making our places more homogenous than ever.

I have a lot more to say about the rut we're in as a profession, but now let's take a break. I need to introduce you, perhaps for the first time, to those for whom we are engaged in planning and design—The Local.

ON BEER AND BEING LOCAL

Outside of a very few cities and towns, most places look like what light beer in a can tastes like to me—watered-down, hum-drum, "just okay" beer that anybody, anywhere, can find. Too many decision-makers in cities play the role of brew master at the light beer brewery—using the meticulously engineered methods and bland ingredients to brew a corporatized, overly-marketed and unremarkable liquid that just "gets the job done."

These days, beer crafters in towns and cities of every size are carefully using local ingredients in small batches to cultivate and extract the tastes of particular cities and neighborhoods. They do this by lovingly selecting local or regional beer-making ingredients. Part of the reason the craft beer movement has exploded is that people generally find the taste and stories behind the making of a geographically-specific local beer to be remarkable. It makes the beverage you're about to enjoy special and unique. When drinking it, you connect with the hops, grain, and yeast. You can imagine being friends or colleagues with the brewer, and you appreciate the craftsmanship involved in the art of the brewing process.

A CRAFT (NOT A CHORE)

Decision makers, like brewmasters, often take the same examples and practices and implement them over and over again, brewing the same plans and just "getting the job done." For too long we have been drinking the flavorless brew because it's easy to find and comforting to drink. We have strayed too far from crafting our plans, our places, and our cities using unique local ingredients.

We need a revolution so that others, when experiencing our places, appreciate the craftsmanship of the decision makers and realize they inhabit a special place. The practice of city planning should embody this kind of art and craftsmanship.

This book was written and published on the wings of the widespread phenomenon underway in the United States and around the world that is based on homegrown, personally-crafted goods and services for The Local. If you've been reading and watching this trend, as I have, you know that this powerful movement is working to counteract globalization and the flattening of global capital and technology. Our cultures, nations, and places are increasingly under this refreshing influence.

More specifically, this movement is also tied to our collective consciousness of environmental sustainability associated with the wasteful practice of transporting goods across the world, a heightened awareness and desire for social equality, and increasing insistence on fair trade agriculture and healthier, organic food. Within this movement is an articulate wave of thinkers, entrepreneurs, and citizen-resistors who are designing for The Local. The most notable of these are designing local economies that integrate alternative models of presentation, consumption, and production. These concepts merge to form the emerging market of consumers that seek local goods and services. Purchasing and consuming local goods acknowledges the uniqueness and artisanal value of regions, hometowns, and familiar neighbors.

WHO IS 'THE LOCAL'?

The Local is a person or group of people—a community or nation—that appreciates the stories behind homegrown products and services. They reject mass-produced, geographically non-specific versions of goods and services. Instead they seek products and services that have stories and a history that remind them of home, or a place like it. Products and services from these places make consumers feel like they are part of the story. The Local is a part of the surrounding community. They have firsthand knowledge and stories of the sacrifices, trials, and tribulations as related to the building of their community's places, businesses, and homes. Locals know the families that produce products and offer services personally as they are considered neighbors. The Local "owns" the pride of production by producing and consuming local goods. The Local therefore more richly participates in the human and physical environments they are a part of. Through this process, The Local belongs.

Many products and services are being designed for The Local, both at a grassroots and at an organized level, and it's happening everywhere. Candles, bicycles, and community farmers markets—virtually anything—can celebrate the traditions associated with specific geographies, particularly their natural resources and climate. Whereas tending to The Local was previously the norm, today, this world of mass production, universal standards, and globalization, which has gained momentum over the past century, is now being questioned and often rejected. The Local is a part of a localization movement, which it sees as exciting and novel because it contrasts sharply with the current economic and cultural systems to which many people have grown accustomed. The Local embraces the localization movement because it's inherently more personal.

OUR REAL CLIENTS

What has generally been missing in this modern push for designing artisan services and homegrown products for The Local is the lack of locally specific communities for locals to enjoy—we generally haven't been creating places that are as geographically-specific and loved as are fresh vegetables locally grown in nearby organic farms. This is a big deal today. For instance, it comes across as strange when I see local beer crafters that are housed in generic, spec-built strip malls that can be found anywhere. The taste and story of local beer, even if it is enjoyed in an ordinary strip mall, ties it to the surrounding hometown; the experience of the physical environment while drinking it might not feel very local at all. This is because, more often than not, too many buildings and spaces that our communities are planning and designing are influenced by global, homogenizing forces that emphasize standardization over uniqueness, local values, and new ideas.

The Local doesn't build and design its own homes or their children's schools—real estate developers and corporatized interests usually do. Developers are in business to make money and they should make money, but like many other for-profit companies, they rely on homogenization, mass production, and standardization. The creation of new developments seems to have fallen under the influence of a Six-Sigma methodology! It's why production home-builders are more concerned with streamlining production than anything else. We care less and less about what the house looks like. We have forgotten how buildings and places contribute to the history and character of our neighborhoods, towns, states, and nations. The only thing too many people care about is how cheap and easy it is to build our places.

I believe that we have entered a new era where The Local is finally beginning to insist on creating special spaces in their communities. Why can't our houses, workspaces, shops, streets, parks, and everything else be as cherished as the products and services we buy and use? Why can't our places be designed and built in a way that is lovingly conceived and artfully crafted? They can and should be! We can utilize a homegrown approach and appeal to The Local to guide the designs of our places. The Local is the missing link to correcting the broken system of urban design. The Local then becomes the inspiration to improve community design and improve our world.

A TRUE GAME CHANGE

I believe that planning and urban design needs a change that can cause the nearly 90,000 municipalities in the U.S. and the hundreds of thousands around the world to embrace The Local. It is only through The Local's creativity that the unique identity or design of a community can take hold.

Until this happens, we'll continue to pave over farms and meadows with more rubber-stamped developments that can be found anywhere. We'll keep making "cute" downtowns together, everywhere, blending one into another, paying no attention to the unique qualities of the cities in which these downtowns are located. We will build homogenous "new urban" subdivisions on the outskirts of cities that attempt to replicate the urban settings of the nearby city. They will feel out of context because they will not pay attention to what makes that outskirt special. Homogenous ideas make our places look and function the same. Such ideas squash economic differentiation and hinder local, regional, and national economic competitiveness.

PLANNING PLAGIARISM

For any game-change vision to be realized, we have to stop copying. Copying ideas is a big reason communities aren't local, and it's what I call "planning plagiarism." Case studies are used by virtually everyone for rationalization and justification. It is unfortunate that, for generations, the most widespread paradigm in placemaking and design has been to copy rather than to create, to design by duplication, and to confuse innovation with imitation. We find what works in another city and think. . .PERFECT! That's exactly what we'll do right here in our city. It's a common and repeated scenario in town after town. This happens every time we "lift" a code by simply changing the original community's name to ours, want and then build another city's big idea, or jump on the latest trendy planning and design bandwagon; we crave formulas.

FEAR AND FORMULAS

As a professor of City and Regional Planning, I am not surprised that we want formulas to help us do our jobs. My students similarly expect easy formulas, which makes me worry about the viability of creative fields. The Local rejects formulas and is involved in creating places worth caring about. Ironically, for students who hope to become city planners, urban designers, and economic development professionals, copying others' work and taking credit for their work is against the rules—well, at least it is while they're in school. Once out, however, working professionals in these fields consider copying others' work and taking credit for their work to be business as usual. The irony is not lost on me. If a student is brazen enough to copy another author's work and try to pass it off as his or her own, then he or she has committed flagrant plagiarism; it's just about the worst thing a student could possibly do. It's a punishable university offense, and students who are found guilty are in jeopardy of being expelled.

Overwhelmingly, I have smart, terrific students, but even my best students often find it hard to think for themselves. This is because too many students have been previously trained to regurgitate the ideas of others; it takes a while before they realize that I really am interested in their ideas.

Many of my new students have a hard time allowing themselves to propose original ideas because they're constantly looking for some kind of universal formula to adhere to in order to earn an A in the course. They'd much rather that I tell them exactly how to think and what to write so they can finish quickly and easily. While precedent is always important when proposing ideas, a lot of students cling to precedent too much. They're more comfortable memorizing someone else's methods than proposing their own. Some students even complain about the courses that I designed to be open-ended and flexible, referring to these kinds of classes as "disorganized." This is because they feel disorganized when asked to think without being given a formula or checklist.

Some students hate to stick their necks out and propose their own bold ideas because they fear being challenged or censured. This is why it would be much easier for me to ask them for an essay on best practices or a history report. I reject this, and I insist that they challenge themselves. It takes time, but eventually, my students leave my class as free-thinking, bold, future shapers of the world's places. Otherwise what's the point of college?

Most professionals and leaders who shape the way our communities look and function seem to share the same fear as my students. Too many of them expect a formula. They want a checklist. They don't want to stick their necks out. They're always pointing to precedent or the law instead of challenging old ideas and creating new laws. They say, "Well, that's how it's always been." So they become content to copy best practices from other places because, they think if the ideas are good, it is probably acceptable to copy.

Meanwhile, their fear, lack of will, lack of imagination, or, most likely, the desire to keep their jobs and retirement programs (which is entirely reasonable) keep them trapped in a rut that has encompassed so many of us in the urban planning profession. All of these things have caused our communities to homogenize and lose their competitive advantage. It's time to encourage each other and educate our leaders and elected officials—who too often hold the creative clamps down on us—to think and to work boldly and innovatively for The Local.

Placemaking professionals are openly encouraged to "plagiarize" ideas. For instance, organizations pushing an agenda almost beg you to "copy this 'smart' code" and apply it in your town so their idea can spread. And, while many of the ideas will serve a greater community good and improve the local quality of life, if many places implement the same ideas, the communities morph into the same boring places. When you attend any city planning or engineering conference, you will hear the term "best practices" used more times than you can count. It's the same in economic development, architecture, and landscape architecture: everyone copies. We should know about, learn from, and go beyond best practices!

We're all guilty. I'm guilty, too. As a planner, I've done it plenty of times in my career. I was asked to "cheat" by my colleagues, my bosses, and the elected officials I served. I have taken ideas and claimed them for the communities that paid my rent. I was praised and even rewarded with promotions and raises. It's part of the scene. It's no wonder that our communities don't stand out, and it's why our neighborhoods look the same and our cities and towns are clones of each other.

THE NAME GAME

While I call it planning plagiarism (although I fully understand it's not technically plagiarism because nobody is getting kicked out of school), many others (it's hard to pinpoint the original coiners of these terms) use "drag and drop planning," "rip-off and replicate planning," and "find and replace planning," and I've also heard the term "cut and paste planning." (Design can be used interchangeably for planning in all of these terms.) I'm sure there have been and will be other names. While we've been naming this practice, generations have passed as communities everywhere continue to "plagiarize" just as much as they have in the past, destroying the true essence of the cultures and histories of places along the way.

The problem with this way of operating is that while implementing a prescription of best practices offers solutions, places eventually look the same, feel the same, and become pretty much the same. Imagine if every local brewery had the same recipe, but varied it slightly after learning it? It may be progress, but the innovation and creativity is lost. We've simply got to stop taking what is unique in one place and making it generic in another. We're creating bland and boring places with nothing new to offer, and we can do better for ourselves.

CHOOSE TO CHANGE

Planning plagiarism is bad for living and bad for business. Thinking anthropologically, when a community blindly accepts any standard that does not tie to local planning craftsmanship, it is either knowingly or unwittingly making a choice to reject its cultural landscape—to take another step toward becoming "just another place." This concept is not new, but thinking about it in this way is fresh. In fact, by now, you probably understand this conversation constitutes a possibility so close to us that most never see it; we need to localize the way we plan and design places. We need to stop plagiarizing, and find a way to change.

REMIX IDEAS

So far, I have accused untold numbers of so-called "placemakers," all with the best intentions for their communities, of being "cheaters" and widget-making robots. But I'm not your fifth-grade teacher. I'm not going to tell you to find a chalkboard and write "I will not cheat again" 500 times. I will contend that it is virtually impossible to design something that can possibly be 100 percent original; it's clear that streets have to have lights and lights usually need poles, and places will probably not want to take the time to reinvent something like street lights and street poles. These things already work well. The same is true for sexually-oriented business clauses that municipalities share. This is also true of sidewalks. Cities build sidewalks because they keep pedestrians safe and they offer high returns on relatively inexpensive municipal investments. If any community ever decides to improve the pedestrian experience with new infrastructure to replace sidewalks and does it in a way that is easy to implement, then it is a sure bet that virtually every other community will want to quickly implement it, too. So, in this way, some sameness is not necessarily bad. Logic therefore also determines the reverse: if it were possible for a community to have everything different, then this, too, might not be good.

MASH THINGS UP

So there are clearly different types of design "plagiarism." A good kind can be in many contemporary artists' works, in which various existing media are mixed and mashed up in various outputs with often-spectacular results. Sometimes the artists even copy, appropriate, and repeat existing works—think about how musicians "sample" other artists' works in entirely fresh ways, creating something new out of something that already exists. Thinking in this way makes it possible for planning to be even more creative. If done well, songs won't feel like a cheaper version that ripped off the original artist. Since virtually nothing is really original, this good kind of copying— referred to in music as a "mash-up"—should be encouraged.

The bad kind of design and planning "plagiarism" involves blindly selecting and plunking down ordinary, widely used designs and plans without an infusion of local character. For instance, the sidewalks mentioned above are good, expected things, but without adding a local twist they contribute to homogeneity. Streetlights taken straight from a landscape architecture catalog do nothing for punching up interest along a corridor—neither does using a "new urban" zoning code and design guidelines from Florida in Wisconsin without replacing "the Florida feel." It isn't enough to replace a few materials.

KEEP PROCESSES

Remixing also means tweaking the planning and design processes. As someone with twenty years of public involvement experience in the public and private sectors and who teaches public involvement at the university level, I am very aware that there are a certain amount of planning and design processes and derivatives of processes that communities can possibly follow. Go ahead and keep following them, but always keep thinking about The Local. Strive to make your buildings and infrastructure uncopyable as a result of the process you choose to pursue. You can do this by making up your mind that you're never going to copy another "bad kind" of placemaking idea again during that process. Never again.

STOP PLANNING TOGETHER

Sharing and implementing the same ideas has been so prevalent over the decades that nearly every community can point to areas of town that were shaped by the city planning, policy, and design fads of years past. These planning and design trends can be compared to music styles, groups, and songs that come and go; they are popular for a period of time and then gradually fade away. The same is true with widely accepted concepts relating to urban planning and design because faddish ideas come and go, but our local landscapes continue to showcase these ideas long after they became obsolete. Illustrating this tendency could fill volumes, but I want to briefly show how widespread copying and sharing has been over time.

URBAN "RENEWAL"

During the mid-1900s, cities embraced the demolition of neighborhoods to make space for the construction of freeways. Seeking to fight declining tax bases, cities throughout the United States embarked on Urban Renewal projects, the ultimate form of planning "plagiarism" in practice. In any city of size, look out for the big, old, impersonal housing projects that appear to have been inspired by Soviet bloc designers. In most locations, these eyesores and disasters for habitation replaced historic neighborhoods. During recent decades, many if not most cities have worked diligently to remedy this mistake. Rather than leveling an historic district in order to build a freeway through the middle of your city, what if your community went its own way and decided to build beautiful parks instead? Or perhaps your city's freeway was so gorgeous it resembled a park? Maybe, instead of eviscerating historic neighborhoods just because of poverty and old houses, a better local solution would have been an attempt to alleviate the poverty and rehabilitate the homes? Or, just imagine if, instead of a just another freeway in yet another city, citizens of your community had come together to devise a new, local method to move people through town. If yours had shown the foresight to innovate instead of imitate, today your city would be a very different place. People would talk about it. It would have a story to tell. It would be a respected model of thoughtful design.

DOWNTOWN STRIP MALLS

In the 1970s and '80s, people continued fleeing the central cities in droves. In response, downtowns everywhere began retrofitting their storefronts to resemble suburban shopping malls by covering the windows, creating blank walls, and covering them over with big, suburban strip-mall-style signs. Evidence of this fad can still be found in downtowns across America. Had business owners simply preserved their buildings, they would not be faced with the costly challenge of retrofitting the buildings back to historic standards generations later.

MCMANSIONS

Generally, the decade from 1990s until the housing crash of 2007 saw the widespread proliferation of "McMansions" that overtook exurban communities. These mass-produced mansions were ordinarily much larger than what a typical family was accustomed to in previous generations. Fringes of our metropolitan communities were overtaken by McMansions. Now all of these places that rushed to embrace this form of development are dealing with the aftermath. The stark reality is that these oversized homes in disconnected neighborhoods are no longer desirable properties for the many young people who are the targeted replacement buyers. Had communities thought about their collective future, they might have prepared themselves differently. Think about how special a community designed by The Local could have become. We relied on an unsustainable national whim, and our cities all did it together.

The previous situations are only three of the many trends that have swept through our cities decade after decade. I can't help but offer a few more:

- 1930s-1960s: one-way streets that fractured historic neighborhoods

- 1950s to today: the loss of historic buildings for parking lots

- 1970s: split-level homes in enormous, residential-only subdivisions

- 1980s to today: first, enclosed malls and later strip malls, big box stores, and fast food restaurants surrounding them

- 1990s to today: gated communities

And most communities have implemented the following together:

- The Big Box

- The Little Box

- Mushroom Buildings (Parking on Bottom Floors)

- The Freeway

- More Freeways

- Widened Freeways

- Suicide Lanes

- Freeway-Sized Streets

- "ET"-era (Wide!) Subdivision Streets

- Tract Houses

- Overly-Engineered Intersections

- Stock Signs

- Historic Demolition

- Strip Malls

- Suburban Sprawl

- Cul-de-Sacs

- Snaky Downtown Streets

- Pedestrian Malls

- Indoor Malls

- Downtown "Malls"

- 1970s Waterfronts

- Leftover Land "Parks" (in Subdivisions)

- Surface Parking Lots

- Buying Catalog Infrastructure

- Drive-Thrus

- Double Drive-Thrus

- Gas Stations Canopies

- Skywalks

- Bad Parking Garages

- One-Way Pairs

- Overhead Lines

- Curb and Gutters

- Suburban Grocery Stores

- Suburban Convenience Stores

- Riprap

- Trailer Parks

- Retail Center Monument Signs

- Chain Link Fences

- Housing "Projects"

- One-Story Buildings (on Urban Corridors)

- Fortified Buildings

- Prisonscapes

- Urban Retail Huts

- Blank Walls

- Cute Downtowns

- Faux Period Structures

- Crappy Buildings with Cheap Siding

- Self-Storage Warehouses

- Art "Hops"/ Walks/Nights

- Bad Water Features

- H.O.V. Lanes

- Skyscrapers

- Billboards

- Service Roads

- Metal Buildings

- Oversized Signs

- Gigantic Monument Signs

- Drive-In Movie Theaters

- Shelterless Bus Stops

- Spaghetti Junctions

- Travel Centers (off freeways)

- Change Copy Signs

- Car Lots

- Reflective Buildings

- Exurban Communities

- Split-Level Houses

- Low-Income Flats

- Water Towers

- Cell Towers

- TV Towers

- Suburban Shrub Landscaping

- Desert Lawns

- 1980s Postmodern Historicism

- Pediments and Columns

- Palladian Windows

- Conventional Subdivisions

- Retaining Walls

- Honey Locust & Vinca Minor

- 1970s Concrete Pots

- 1980s Globe Streetlights

- Separated Land Uses

- Late-20th-Century Transit Center Architecture

I understand the arguments against designing local and for standardization. (For instance, I know communities are physical organisms that experience similar situations that can call for universal solutions.) I also understand that some things we enjoy about our communities could have been a planning and design best practice in previous decades. I accept that being human means keeping up with fads and trends. Regardless, just with these few examples, it should be clear that jumping on the same planning and urban design bandwagon causes indistinguishable places. Parcel by parcel and building by building—when we plan together, we become the same.

STOP PLANNING TOGETHER

MUSICAL CHAIRS

As a result of fad-following, our cities are essentially playing musical chairs with development. We use and discard land based on flavor-of-the-month fads. We decide that after one place has been developed, we should move on to the next. In our current game of musical chairs winners and losers are the local economy. The old, now "bad" areas of town (the dated losers that were a part of a past development era) are replaced by new, "good" areas of town (the contemporary winners), and the cycle continues. This phenomenon is even more startling when considering the concept of town centers. Often placemakers argue that only through development of new town-centers can we wrangle and control development, yet in the process of plagiarism we designate new town-centers that look like old ones while simultaneously abandoning our previous town-centers. This insanity is unsustainable.

While "plagiarism" is often practiced with good intentions, such as the pursuit of diversity and equality, in virtually any metro area diversity and equality are not achieved through this kind of "planning." These new, desirable places we're building are enabled by those at the high end of the income spectrum. These places have the strongest real estate values, the best-educated citizens, and in most cases, they usually have the strongest economies and the most robust coffers. Almost universally, the areas of town that are the most desirable also have the strongest design ethics. Test this out where you are.

If our communities would plan for The Local and not for what's in fashion at the time, we could eliminate the unsustainable musical chairs game most of our communities play. It's as if there is some grand conspiracy afoot in which the Godfather real estate developers, urban planners, and engineers get together every few years to decide in secret what the next cockamamie new thing will be!

I am joking here, but in all seriousness, as a concerned citizen, I am often astounded by the lack of ingenuity involved in what we are supposed to be doing. There has to be some plausible reason that we all seem to be waiting for the next "Big Thing" to be handed down to us. It's a huge problem.

STOP WORSHIPPING OTHER CITIES

To plan and design for The Local, I believe that one giant positive step for cities to take would be to stop worshipping other cities by attempting to imitate them. Throughout my career, several places in particular have been referenced countless times. In the United States, a few cities tend to do things first. They adopt new ideas first. Then these ideas trickle down to other cities. These are the Godfather cities, providing protection from creativity to cities across the country. As a planner, I, too, have great respect for these "first-adopter cities," as do so many others in my field. I wanted to obtain for my city what they have acquired for theirs. I liked to insert these cities in conversations as much as possible. I read their local newspapers and local blogs, researched their local "vibe," and even visited these cities to see what being a local looked and felt like. Looking back, I was naïve.

THE SECRET

If you think about it, it is clear these first-adopters aren't really even first-adopters. Their dirty secret: they copy as much as your city does, and what they copy seems more interesting until everyone has it. For instance, second-adopter cities have long been copying ideas such as painting bicycle lanes blue. The idea of painting bike lanes blue didn't come from the first-adopter city, but a pre-first adopter city that was focused on solving a very real problem. It then became a best practice, but all the individuality of the original idea has been lost; if a "first-adopter" city did it, cities everywhere soon will have bike lanes painted blue.

BEWARE OF WIDGETS

Widget-based design and implementation makes sense if you are building 10,000 replica Dodge Chargers. Nobody wants any surprises when you are buying a new car. Widget-based formulas are vital to a heart surgeon's complicated procedures because she needs to perfect a quadruple-bypass surgery and keep the patient alive. Widget-based physics is also critical for engineers whose responsibility is to get an astronaut up into space and safely back down to Earth. But places, like people, beg to be unique. They are supposed to be emotive because they are founded by people, and people are emotional. They want to evoke responses. Think of a world where every person looked and acted the same. It would be a terrible world. But that's the kind of world we're building for places. Achieving a unique, emotive, and responsive community is impossible if we're using widget-based design.

OUR BIBLES KEEP US IN LINE

It seems as though we're all building the same things: widgets. And, as a result, we're generally morphing into the same place: widgets. We're all designing from the same manuals, too. For instance, The *AASHTO Design Guides* with universal formulas, dimensions, and materials dictates what civil engineers think they have the right to design. Common street designs are in this manual. You don't have to think; you just pull out the design. I can only dream that civil engineers will decide to have a conversation about their impact on individual communities, and the impact of widget-based design on these communities.

I fear that engineers in charge of infrastructure have not been taught to think comprehensively about how these universal specs are causing places to become indistinguishable; instead, I believe that most of them are generally concerned only with how fast the traffic flows and how the overall system functions. I know this is important, too. But while safety standards are paramount (we need to make sure the car stays on the curve of a road, for example), we do not necessarily need universal design standards for all infrastructure projects. Safety does not necessarily equate with universality.

Why do apartment mailboxes have to be so dull? I bring this up because apartment mailboxes are infrastructure that can be seen on the ground. They are everywhere in cities and in suburbia, and sometimes they can be found in stand-alone kiosks within parking lots. Picture an apartment mailbox in your mind: a huge box of rectangular boxes with a small rectangular hole cut out for a particular apartment dweller's name and a key hole. I'm sure you recognize this design. It and many other parts of our places have been cloned an untold number of times directly from *Architectural Graphics Standards*, also known as the "architect's bible."

Urban and regional planners also have a couple of their own "bibles." One is called *The Practice of Local Government Planning*, which is simply referred to as "the green book." The other is *Planning and Design Standards*, known as "the blue book." These big, dry books teach planners about existing tools for planning communities, most notably referencing zoning codes and standard designs, the law, and precedent. And while these books are not as prescriptive as The *AASHTO Design Guides* and *Architectural Graphics Standards*, and while the ideas are very good, I believe that it promotes a kind of herd mentality that resembles widget-based thinking.

PERFECT WIDGETS

A famous park that has become one of the most popular "widget parks" began as an elevated railroad spur. Once upon a time it provided a solution to a problem in a major metropolitan city that suffered from pedestrian and automobile congestion. The project didn't expect to become a media sensation, but in the time since its implementation it has been hailed as a monumental success. It's been written about all over the world. With that type of success it easily enters into the best practice books and opens up the possibility that it will be plagiarized by other city planners. Other neighborhoods in the same city and others around the country and throughout the world began contemplating their own version of this park. Soon every city will have a park on an elevated railroad spur. It's a pre-packaged solution. All we have to do is implement it! It's a planning widget.

The above example, as stunning and inspirational as it is, is a perfect mold for additional planning widgets. It's formulaic. It works easily; it's very tangible. It can be implemented by using a linear thought process that can be absorbed by the professional masses in an easy ABC formula, whereas:

A = AN OLD, ABANDONED, ELEVATED RAILWAY

+

B = A LINEAR PARK

=

C = PARK AND ELEVATED RAIL WIDGET

(ANOTHER PERFECT WIDGET)

I call this kind of simple formula the Perfect Widget for professionals. It's easy to understand and apply. If anyone is skeptical or confused over the ideas, all that's needed is a field-trip to the city where the perfect widget example has been implemented. Upon visiting, we clearly see how well it's working and then reasonably deduce that it is, in fact, a low-risk project.

ALL KINDS OF WIDGETS

Other widgets that many cities adopt and adapt to are landmarks or festivals. Whereas many of the cities with the "first ideas" have things that were created and fostered by locals, too many Greek-looking buildings from non-Greek countries, pieces of non-indigenous modern art, Times Square-like intersections, music festivals, sporting events, holiday parades, Fourth of July fireworks, holiday celebrations like St. Patrick's Day, Oktoberfest, and Mardi Gras exist in places they don't fit. Often times, first-adopter cities or those with the cultural heritage to support such a festival or landmark, do such a good job that another city thinks that they can do even better.

Now, many cities across the U.S. seem to be starting their own "Running with the Bulls." They want each of the festivals to be complete with the same people, atmosphere, and giveaways as the one they're borrowing from. Then they fail and wind up being an event that a lot of people ridicule.

Instead, let the signature landmark or festival come to you through embracing The Local nature of your city. At some point that is exactly what happened in the city your community took its Widget from. While it may have started as something small, and others copied it after seeing its success, your city believes it can still embrace and improve it.

Another Widget is the Naming Widget. Take, as only one example, "The Friendly City." There are many "Friendly Cities" in the United States. In fact, there are at least six U.S. states that have "Friendly Cities" of their own. I doubt that these places are in competition with each other to determine which is the friendliest, but it further exposes the problem of homogeneity. Another similar problem begs the question:

how can a city possibly be "weird" if it copies slogans from other cities? A city in Texas claimed it was weird before a handful of follower cities went about trying to make it their own, too.

B randing efforts, when copied, do the opposite of providing a unified message. Most of the copies fall flat and are subject to similar ridicule, and often they hurt the entity being branded. While it is difficult to suddenly become original, you should not spend time defining your town with slogans, because they're just not terribly effective. It is marketing panache that doesn't pay the promised dividends.

A doption of slogans also further illustrates the problem of formulas. It's hard to turn down formulas that have worked for other places, like being a friendly city or a weird place, but this is certainly not planning for The Local. Words matter. When places can't even come up with an original slogan, it's a sign that its buildings and infrastructure look and function the same way they do in other communities.

It's no wonder that it is increasingly hard to tell one place from another. Don't define yourself through the Naming Widget.

AN ETHICAL PRACTICE

If you happen to be a certified planner in the United States you may not know that widgets are very much frowned on by the American Planning Association's AICP Code of Ethics and Professional Conduct. Section 1 (Our Overall Responsibility to the Public) of Part A: "Principles to Which We Aspire" states, *"We shall promote excellence of design and endeavor to conserve and preserve the integrity and heritage of the natural and built environment."* Section 2, (Our Responsibility to Our Profession and Colleagues) mandates that, *"We shall examine the applicability of planning theories, methods, research and practice and standards to the facts and analysis of each particular situation and shall not accept the applicability of a customary solution without first establishing its appropriateness to the situation."* In other words, we should already be designing local!

ECONOMIC DEVELOPMENT

Universities hope students will fall in love as much with the surrounding community as with the campus itself, so they will be more inclined to enroll. CEOs and startup entrepreneurs often decide to locate their businesses in a city based on the "vibe" of a place and the uniqueness of a particular address. Visitors and tourists want to stop and spend time and money in the most noteworthy local communities.

While many communities are already great as a result of the people who live there, they need to solidify their futures as places where people want to live, create, visit, and spend money. Building individual communities based on blueprints virtually ensures that local economic development playing fields become leveled by allowing themselves to become cookie-cutter versions of every other place. It's really simple, and simply a matter of money.

DESIGN IS POWERFUL

An enormous challenge in the vast majority of our communities is that aesthetics, urban design, and the very idea of "placemaking" are generally looked on as non-essential, low-priority, "fluffy" subjects. However, convention dollars are not fluffy. Consider how people choose their vacations. They certainly do not choose to spend their hard-earned money and limited time to visit an unremarkable place. People like to share photos of interesting things from out-of-the-ordinary places, not ordinary places. People working in creative fields surely don't dream about locating a business in a ho-hum place. They want to be associated with expressive places that match their ingenuity. It should ring clear by now that authentic local design, which tells an effective local story, is a potential form of powerful economic development.

THE STORIES WE'RE TELLING

Storytelling in planning and urban design is based on the premise that every place has an interesting story to tell—stories filled with special people, individual histories, and particular aspirations. Many great books and valuable scholarly journal articles have been published on this subject too, though most are either unknown and/or unread by the people who most need to read them. Perhaps this is why so many of our communities don't know how to or why they should strive to properly implement good local stories in their landscapes because the best stories are local, the best local stories are authentic, and authentic places are cherished.

It's because of this that authentic places are high on the itineraries of vacationers. These cities are destinations because they're etched on to the human psyche as special destinations that we all know. And, they are all recognized, at least in part, because of the details—design feature details that exist on the ground. These details—famous street corners, famous sidewalks, lighted boulevards, and signs—all contribute to the overall feeling, character, and story of the place.

STORYTELLING

Streets can tell stories, as can storefronts, signage, buildings, parks, restaurant booths, staircases, and roadside attractions. For example, stories that portray a longtime owner and founder of a neighborhood coffee shop who kept the place open for 50 successful years now can be displayed in a sidewalk-facing window. When visitors understand "the authentic story" of a place, especially after experiencing it themselves, they spread the story by telling others about their experience. They also encourage others to go and "hear the story" for themselves.

Through authentic local storytelling, places can finally shine with their own light instead of looking like each other. The success is in the details!

Some cities pull stories together very well. Consider a city where there is a world-famous auditorium home to a unique form of music. The stage, made of manicured pinewood planking, tells the story of the music legends who once stood on that very spot. You'll be drawn to walk the streets and alleys filled with dive bars and seedy corners, feeling and experiencing the ghosts of a legend's ambition, success, and heartache. All of the local history is converging in this place—and you dream of being able to tell new stories of hopeful, budding stars of tomorrow who frequent the record stores, bars, and coffee shops. You'll imagine where famous singers sang on the sidewalks for change, and drink a beer at the bar where another got into a drunken fight, or stay in the hotel that was once trashed by a legend of the musical genre. Perhaps you'll shop at the boutique where they bought their dress or suit for their first major awards show.

Visit the cemetery to pay respects to an icon, or a forgotten star. Or, you can simply enjoy the broader story of the very concept of the music in the city itself and delight in the icons, the lights, and the sounds. This oozes from the urban design aesthetic. The physical environment has been designed to tell its story to the world.

BUILDING, NOT BRANDING

Please recognize that, at least in the traditional sense, I am not talking about "branding." Branding is not usually a ground-up approach; therefore it is not usually an authentic process, especially when it occurs inorganically. When determining a brand, how does a city back up a new bold claim? If its landscape doesn't match the new story it wants to tell, then the branding effort will fail. Your city's proclamation will fall on deaf ears and the inauthentic story will be forgotten and the taxpayers' dollars will be wasted.

NO PRETENSES

You should never try to make your neighborhoods be like a currently famous neighborhood, and if you want to try to be like one, you've already failed. This way of thinking is one of the reasons too many of our communities are not authentic. In other words, the Story Widget is not a good placemaking strategy. It's not enough to say that "what works in City XYZ will surely work here." Most places are having a terrible time cultivating their stories. For as long as most of us have been alive our communities have been buried under generic things that inhabit our living spaces. This makes storytelling hard.

HOW TO TELL A BETTER STORY

How can a better story be told about your city, town, or neighborhood? The good news is that your city already *is* a story! The stories are there, waiting to be told in a way that will define it as an amazing place. Instead of traditional branding or trying to be somewhere else, cities should spend time shaping their story, site by site, building by building. We need to be sensitive to The Local by letting the story tell itself through the design decisions on which its residents agree. The best stories are cultivated organically.

Building an organic consensus of your citizens—in other words, working with The Local— will help your city extract its essence. It's only then that you can believe that every part of a place—from the street pavement and the fountain to the parking lot—tells a story. You need to understand that each of these parts combine to tell the collective story of the community. Most places have done an absolutely dreadful job in telling their special story, and we are all to blame. This is because for too long we have ignored The Local and favored the Widget.

After many years of thinking about and researching this topic I'm convinced that good planning ultimately involves creative storytelling through design. Like all ideas, this one has been around for a very long time, but it's a concept that is generally ignored in municipal staff reports, comprehensive plans, and the everyday practice of planning. As planners, we're too busy following what our zoning codes say and we don't think enough about how unique places are directly connected to the age-old practice of storytelling. It's hard for us to comprehend that stories always get told whether you choose to tell your own relevant stories or whether you allow others (such as corporations and engineers) to tell their own stories for your community. If your community ever hopes to see culturally relevant development built on the ground, it must first understand this relationship and why it is important.

TACOS

To better illustrate this point, please choose between these tacos:

- A taco prepared by a chain that you pick up in a drive-through building. The taco is prepared by a high school student working part-time in a small city, or

- A taco made in a specially-built, authentic hacienda made of real stucco and real terra cotta, from a family recipe handed down over 100 years and prepared by the family matriarch.

I'm sure you chose the authentic taco. There's a much better, more authentic story there. Maybe it's the story of how the owner of the restaurant, a grandmother, started making her now-famous tacos that are loved by thousands. For many decades, the grandmother sprinkled love into each tortilla, as she carefully prepared her delicious, spicy-authentic taco featuring her secret guacamole recipe that was handed down, in the strictest confidence, from her great grandmother more than 60 years ago. She is making sure this proud taco tradition reaches her own great grandchildren, and her deepest yearning is that the tacos are made in exactly the same way years from now as they have been for the last 60. This story, pointing to a taco's proud history, has to be more interesting—more remarkable—than a kid trying to make video game money stuffing ground beef filling and cheese into a mass-produced shell in an everyday chain store that looks like thousands of others. However, even if that taco is made by the high school student instead of the grandmother, the building itself is more fun and remarkable than just another old chain drive-through if the local context makes sense for it to exist.

MATERIAL CULTURE

Most places have no interest in banning chain fast-food restaurants, or for that matter any other chain store coming to town. I agree with this. These businesses have every right to locate on private property, and the company buys properties everywhere. But every community absolutely has the right to determine how these buildings contribute to its material culture.

Material culture is an anthropological term that often refers to artifacts and their meaning. A drive-thru chain store will be an artifact someday. A big-box sign could be dug up and analyzed in future times. Consider then, that everything humans put on the ground becomes—in fact already is— material culture, and what we build points to who we are as a people and defines what we value. This is why everything we build or implement—a particular color and texture of brick, a bike rack, a gas station canopy— determines who we are. Each community must understand why demanding locally-significant development and infrastructure is meaningful, and that it adds value to the local story because it tells its own, new story that is relevant to the area. Unfortunately, most places are not prepared for when it's time for a corporation to present their expected design that offers nothing special to a community rather than celebrating that company's values.

NICE IS NOT ENOUGH

It's important to distinguish between nice places and places that celebrate local values. I know that when I travel to another city for a convention, I want to be in a place that I can brag about to my friends back at home. I want an experience. An annual meeting held in a nice (but entirely ordinary) city is not very exciting. So, even though you may not be a big fan of what a city has to offer, I'm sure you picked the one with the more interesting, attractive, or exciting material culture. You can tell your friends that you're going to a place that has a distinctive ambience, and most of your friends will be impressed. They can tell their own stories about what they think about the culture of that city, too. Few people can tell any stories about a featureless community.

It's no wonder why large conventions return to the same handful of cities over and over. For instance, the professional organization to which I belong, the American Planning Association, has recycled good storytellers such as Chicago, Boston, New Orleans, and Washington, DC, even though there are many more cities that can accommodate the group and wait to be explored. I understand that big conferences need big city infrastructure and ample hotel rooms that can only be provided by a few cities, but let's be honest, not many of us would want to part with our hard-earned money on an unknown commodity, and this includes any unknown or otherwise generic city. This is also true for corporations, entrepreneurs, and folks who just want a change of scenery in a new city.

Many off-the-radar places are considered to be, generically speaking, "nice." Maybe they're "clean." Or perhaps they're "safe," or a combination of these. While few would argue the virtues of living in a place that is nice, clean, and safe, these communities act as though they have nothing else to offer. If your community is one of these kinds of places, especially if it's in a cold climate, or lacks natural visual amenities, or apparent cultural attractions, it must become amazing, fascinating, and therefore "worth visiting again," as well as nice and clean. Nice is simply not enough. I can't say this enough!

JUST GIMME MY GENERIC DRUGSTORE

Midway during my writing I took some time for a reconnaissance trip to research the design of a particular chain of drug stores, although I could have chosen any kind of store in order to tell this story. All the 15 stores in 15 communities I visited were beige-colored synthetic stucco on the outside, with a deep building set back from the road and surrounded by prominent parking lots. Their major distinguishing feature was the windows on the front corner of the store, or the portico. There were slight but insignificant variations of two square windows on all of the stores. Older stores I visited were shorter and without porticos.

But they were the same beige color, were coated in familiar synthetic stucco, had the same rectangular windows, and were also set back from the street by a giant parking moat. Whereas some did have minor differences, for example, terra cotta shingles on one store and landscaping in the front of another, the stores were almost always identical, and intentionally so.

FAMILIAR COMMODITIES

I'm sure you're not surprised by any of this. After all, chain stores are purposefully designed to be easily cloned to make them cheaper when they are built in a variety of locations. They are commodities placed in communities by investors. More importantly, these cloned designs exist so customers can recognize their company brands, which are partly established by the design of their buildings. It is in the best interest of companies to create a familiar experience for their customers, who may be traveling to other cities and want to find and use their services. They want to know what to expect and what they are going to get. This is entirely reasonable. We all need the same things in our communities that can sustain human life and our collective well-being: water, food, transportation, places to shop, schools, hospitals, homes, and parks. But they don't have to be widgets. I understand the clear benefits of not being surprised and "knowing what you get" when you see a gasoline company sign: "gasoline ahead!" If you like chicken and pizza and you're traveling, I understand that it can be beneficial to know by the very shape of a building's roof that there is delicious fried chicken or pizza inside. What I don't understand is why all of these communities allow these generic stores to be built in the first place? My experience tells me that too many municipalities think these drugstores and fast food restaurants are a godsend, needed for jobs, growth, and to provide services for their residents. The serious business of jobs calls for numbers and flow-chart politics. Meetings about placement of these rubber-stamp retail sites lead decision-makers to believe that jobs do not rely on aesthetics but on the hard information that lies in front of them. Community character is cast to the wayside in order to serve the more immediate and pressing need for modern commerce.

FREEDOM AND HERITAGE

Yet communities that are rejecting generic building designs and working to uncover an authentic community have been able to change the appearances of these drug stores. Designing for The Local means that urban planners and other decision-makers work with the corporate entity not only to preserve the corporate image and the familiar nature of the store, but also to enhance it by improving the community and allowing its residents to take pride in their own handiwork. Some places wrongly consider design rules to be akin to communism, as in, "It's not right to dictate how businesses should look in a free country or tell a property owner what to do with his property." But locals know how best to determine what their community should look like and how it should function. This is far from communism; it's "local determinism" and it embraces The Local. It's homegrown freedom, it's fighting for your community, and it's realizing that yours can end up favored and appreciated over the community next door.

So when a generic drugstore is proposed near your home, instead of thinking "Great! Now, when I want to go there I won't have to drive too far," let your response be, "Let's make sure this contributes to our cultural heritage." Or at the very least, "Let's see if we can make it say 'home' and 'ours' a little better."

REALITY

S o far it may have seemed as though I have been very hard on chain stores, and hopefully the dutiful reader has, to this point, understood that I am not suggesting that places eliminate chain stores; in fact, I am an appreciative patron of several chain stores, as are an overwhelming majority of consumers. I am not protesting corporations. It's important for me to stress that although I would absolutely rather live in a world filled with caring local merchants with interesting local products, I would never suggest that your community go to the extreme of attempting to legally ban chain stores and replace them with only mom-and-pop stores.

Whereas I am aware of the good reasons for supporting a return to mom-and-pop shopping, I believe that dealing with reality is necessary and inspires innovation. Our world is filled with millions who like to shop at big-box grocery and hardware stores, generic drugstores, and fast food chains. Chain stores are here to stay. Again, please don't miss my point: communities can decide to design their landscapes in such a way as to reflect their local culture and local values—values that are particular to that one spot on Earth—and therefore have the power to differentiate that particular spot on Earth from any other. I believe that places don't have to become a collection of the same commonly expected and widespread designs and widgets found nearly everywhere. This holds true no matter what type of business is proposed, whether it is a national chain or an independently owned business. The Local can influence them all.

It's time for The Local to step up and change the trajectory by prohibiting unfortunate communities to proliferate in the future.

REALITY

WHISKEY TOWN THREATENED

Whiskey Town is a village with a strong history and a coherent story: it is the hometown of one of the world's most famous whiskey brands. No other town can ever claim to be the one-and-only home of this most celebrated whiskey. Although the whiskey distillery located there is every bit a corporate entity, the feel of the town is anything but. This is a big reason why, for many visitors, Whiskey Town is a fantastic day-trip, particularly the rustic, oaky flavor of the local design that is found on and immediately around the town's square. It's a wonderfully original destination.

Local businesses on the town square do a great job of exploiting a unique whiskey aesthetic. By placing whiskey-based placards on the windows, using whiskey barrels in the façades, and demonstrating their part in the history of the distillery, businesses communicate the history and flavor of their town to visitors. These tourists can see how the whiskey stored in the old warehouses perched on the hills above the town worked to create a place that isn't replicable anywhere in the world. The village lets the visitor in on the secret stories of the prohibition era through an inviting old-fashioned personality.

Cameras work overtime as friends and family visitors make sure to capture the experience of rustic, whiskey-filled Whiskey Town, and all along the square you often hear people talking in foreign languages. People come from around the world to experience Whiskey Town.

As a whole, Whiskey Town's commercial square is an excellent example of the power of designing for The Local. There's a clear story. And even though whiskey could be considered Whiskey Town's brand, it doesn't seem fake or forced because whiskey has long been a part of the community.

Nothing is overdone. Whiskey Town exploits its special attributes in an authentic way; it doesn't feel like a trip to the faux Main Street in Disneyland. The place is remarkable. It's worthy of telling others about it.

A s perhaps the smallest town in the region with the most robust story and character, part of the charm of a trip to Whiskey Town is that it is itself. It's different. But this town's special attributes are being threatened. Sadly, a community bank on the southeastern corner of the town square has been covered with a stucco-type material that smothers the aesthetic. It destroys the rhythm that is created by the other buildings and that contributes to the overall experience. This bank is not photo-worthy. It's not special. It tells no story. It's hard to imagine what the cultural and economic impact would be if the entire square was plastered over with this character-flattening stucco material. According to Whiskey Town's rules, there is nothing keeping stucco from invading the rest of the buildings.

B eyond the stucco-plastered bank, the essence of Whiskey Town is being threatened by several developments that are beginning to encroach on the special character of the community. A metal warehouse storage facility, a few generic strip malls, and a drug store that looks like it could be anywhere are all too close to the square for comfort. These cheap-looking and non-contributing structures can be found in nearly any community; they are especially out-of-place in the middle of Whiskey Town.

It's possible that the special "Whiskey Town feeling" that day-trippers expect could be all but eliminated if a burst of new commercial services began to emerge like weeds in a garden plot. The town's rustic ambience could succumb to common design elements like strip malls and fast food signs.

Whiskey Town is not far away from booming metropolitan regions and is especially close to a fast growing city. It's because of this that it is not inconceivable that Whiskey Town, one of the most iconic communities in the entire world, would be the next town to experience tremendous development pressure. If it takes a passive stance on planning and design, it is, in effect, permitting itself to become like so many other towns that have blindly allowed generic metal buildings, ordinary-looking structures, and chain restaurants to stamp their own stories on to otherwise distinctive locales. If it is to thrive, Whiskey Town must retain its unique local design; it must continue to tell its distinctive story, which, ironically, is defined by an internationally-recognized corporation that happens to be local.

If the essence of Whiskey Town disappears, its economy will be threatened; people want to visit a remarkable place, not just another ordinary town. It needs to act decisively to protect its unique character, perhaps through clear design expectations that define and celebrate the town's heritage. Your community should too.

STREET TALK

Perhaps the single most influential factor in determining the look and feel of a community is its streets. For example, here is what is common for most of us: a four-lane street with a turn lane in what I will call Anytown. As the main thoroughfare in Anytown this corridor was once a two-lane road with gentle curves, green pastures, and local businesses, all of which combined to create a pastoral experience that was representative of the region.

This country road was widened into a new five-lane highway, transforming the look and feel of what was a small country village. Many of us are from an area like this, and we know that the new highway is often viewed as an upgrade by locals. Now, however, drivers can pass through town without blinking an eye; there is no need to slow down and experience the community.

G rowth is generally looked upon favorably by many if not most communities, but I find this transformation to be a shame. Sure, cars can now easily pass each other. That's great. But before the five-lane highway was constructed, Anytown seemed more like an interesting place to be, instead of a place to rush past. Today, although the town has its own history, stories, and aspirations, which are specific to its proud people and its particular geography, the "upgraded" generic street design has created a speedway landscape that makes it much more difficult to tell the local story. This is because Anytown doesn't resemble a tiny pastoral community anymore, even though it still is.

W hen people think of the interesting small village of Anytown, they likely think of narrow, winding roads, or quaint corridors, not five-lane freeways with "stripped out commercial" land that can be found in mega suburbs and in big cities.

The new five-lane street doubles as a small scale freeway whose priority is a destination farther down the road, rather than the town's main commercial street, where most of its businesses are located, and to which most drivers are simply oblivious as they barrel through. The new "strip" attracts the telltale prototype businesses that severely homogenize communities.

Anytown became generic by design, but you'd never know that, for example, some of the richest farmland is minutes away or that a scenic river, one of the most important in the region for the biodiversity of native aquatic species, runs nearby. It's hard to see anything here that is special along the road; and the new standard street design will call for ordinary suburban commercial strip development featuring—no surprise here— big box chain stores, gas stations, strip malls, and prototypical fast food restaurants.

What's troubling with this example is that, no matter what existed on the street before reconstruction began— whether it was historic homes, interesting buildings that tell stories of the people who once inhabited them, a big stand of trees that existed before the town did, or any other notable landmarks—these standard, generic, fast designs are often considered by engineers and citizens alike as more important to carry through to implementation than is a tree or an old house. Since five lane streets are everywhere, community character is inundated in their wake. All that needs to be done is to lay the standard plan on top of the existing right-of-way; never mind that the corridor will look like all the others. In the guise of "progress," the new street will obliterate the character—muting the story the community once told—just to allow cars to move faster and to create an environment conducive to the building of strip malls.

STREETS IN THE WORLD'S COUNTRIES

Unfortunately, growing evidence suggests that all cities and towns across the world are similarly vulnerable to losing the special qualities that make their places unique in exchange for corporate recognition and convenience. The Local is increasingly concerned with the material cultural heritage in developing countries, especially as it relates to highway infrastructure. For example, many "highways" in foreign lands are memorable, remarkable experiences. These roads often do not feature paint (either on the sides or in the middle to separate the lanes).

For many non-natives, driving along such roads is exciting, because there are surprises—narrowing and widening points in and out of the savannas and jungles, intimate bridges worthy of stopping for a photo, and places where it is necessary to slow down to pass pedestrians and cyclists who share the road. On the "highway" it's possible to pull over and eat lunch on the river without the assistance of an exit ramp or a traffic light. It's truly a remarkable experience that constitutes a singular reason to make a special trip because the highway does a great job exposing tourists to the authentic culture of the place. This material cultural landscape includes virtually nothing, save a familiar brand of gas station here and there, that is based on standard designs.

Whereas there are plenty of ways this highway could be improved for safety,

I fear that it and others like it will be eventually influenced by standard engineering, and, if that happens, the highway will resemble the one that was designed for Anytown. It will lose a feature that makes for rich, authentic storytelling. Unfortunately, this is the story of the United States. Before the highway revolution created by the Eisenhower Interstate System and an increasingly streamlined civil engineering standard, many highways and streets in the country offered a rich, local experience similar to that still found abroad.

STREET NOSTALGIA

If you think of the mystique of 1950s-style cross-country road trips along dusty thoroughfares, a scene that still exists in many people's minds, you're probably in an antique convertible whizzing down the road filled with Americana kitsch and flavor. In fact, old two-lane bridges throughout the U.S., while not likely original to those particular bridges along such corridors, are otherwise intimate and reminiscent of the charming "highways" described above in other countries.

Across-country trip used to mean appreciating and absorbing regional and local heritage as you moved west or east. This kind of experience still exists in many off-the-beaten path highway routes as can still be found in some areas, but it has largely faded in the U.S. While it's true that U.S. citizens enjoy the convenience and predictability that is provided by "first-world" highway and street infrastructure, its overly engineered design is not suited to the kind of marvelous experience that, say, many "less developed" countries offer.

BEYOND FAMILIAR

I understand that street design and implementation is more complicated than what I just described, but not too much more. I'm also guessing that a lot of readers (maybe you) believe that I am ignoring the importance of familiarity and consistency for drivers. It's a great argument! Surely it's prudent to reassure as many drivers as possible that no matter where they go they'll be able to maneuver the middle turn-lane (popularly known as the "suicide lane") of a five-lane street as safely as possible. It's important that we all become experts at accelerating the on-ramps correctly, and if you've attempted one on-ramp you can maneuver them all. We also are thankful that green means go. However, many a "spec" street design that has proliferated throughout many continents has been detrimental to community character. This includes a standard design for alleys, residential streets, collector and arterial streets, freeways, overpasses—even traffic signs and crosswalk signals. In fact, just about every new street on the ground was implemented from Widget-based designs.

LEARN TO SAY "NO"

We also have to teach our communities to say "No!" The more stalwart and sustainable communities became that way by paying attention to their design. One way this was accomplished was by saying "No!" to unwanted, badly designed development proposals, even though doing so is often contrary to what most municipalities want to believe. In communities with few resources and few retail services, a challenge to, say, a big retail box's boilerplate design is probably considered unthinkable and politically disastrous.

Just imagine the impact of this development pulling out and locating in an adjacent community: Future taxes lost! Future employment opportunities disappeared! And, perhaps worst of all—an egg on your town's face. It shouldn't and doesn't have to be this way.

I believe that professionals who have a hand in shaping places are meant to have inspired jobs. If you agree, and if you're in one of those professions, ask yourself if you went into your field to rubber stamp burger joint permits for basic buildings that can be found virtually everywhere. Was the time and trouble you took to become an elected official or any other involved position worth it if you ended up making your city invisible in the process? For the sake of creating remarkable places instead of clones of each other, we all must commit to becoming visionaries instead of bureaucrats. We have to elevate our profession and the way society sees us.

Citizens also have responsibilities. Citizens who care about their neighborhoods must hold leaders to higher standards and expect only special things be built in their communities. Remember that public servants work for the people. Their jobs are in place to make citizen's lives better. It's my hope that local leaders will think twice before approving the same buildings, highways, houses, schools, stores, parks, and restaurants that many other places do in large part because the designers and planners have their noses in the same manuals. However, they will only innovate if The Local insists they do. It's The Local's responsibility to remind professionals and decision-makers to establish their own local playbooks so that the place that citizens care about can stand out from the rest and become competitive.

GUIDELINES NOT TEMPLATES

A lot of communities have some design controls they call guidelines that act more like templates because most of them have been shared by numerous municipalities that seek a common aesthetic. (For example, wanting to be a "nice suburban community.") In other words, they're usually the result of best practices that have been distributed and adopted nearly universally. Shared or lifted templates explain why there are so many nice suburban communities with fine things that can be found just about anywhere. Design templates may offer a few simple tweaks from place to place, such as, for example, a bigger stucco portico and extra landscaping around an otherwise generic drug store.

What I propose is for each community to chart its own destiny, and this takes more imagination than fixed design rules.

In order for this to happen, locals have to be on board with planning as a design tool and not just a land use tool. They have to insist on quality architecture and design imagination. They must demand cultural relevance and push cultural norms at the same time. They have to ensure that good decision-making in local development tells the right story, makes an impact, and—in the best word that sums up the desired result—is remarkable. When this happens, our citizens will feel more pride in their communities. If every community took the time to establish such individual standards, it would be much easier to know where we are, and, therefore, be able to make choices about where we live, shop, and visit.

THE CALL

I trust that by now you see how designing special places cannot be achieved by just lifting ideas from one place and dropping them in your community. It can't be based on some national bandwagon that will come and go sooner or later, or followed by some other trendy widget idea that every place rushes to implement. You cannot let someone else "more important" do your thinking for you, and you can't be suckered into falling for some new "model ordinance" just because neighboring towns have adopted it. At this point, you should clearly see how we design places like widgets on an assembly line, resulting in indistinguishable, interchangeable, and dreadfully boring communities. You know that boring is bad for living and is bad for business.

I recognize that I have offered your community a tremendous challenge. I know that, unfortunately, most people have become so accustomed to widget-like places that they don't demand unique ones.

As I mentioned, there are about 90,000 municipalities in the United States, thousands more in Canada, Mexico, and Central America and probably a few million others around the world, and most can't—or won't—think, much less design, for themselves by embracing The Local. Many have lost their way. I'm calling for a new era of designing places that we enjoy living in, and that encourages unique views and new life for the community you care about. Designing local is based on local pride and local ideas. Only through embracing your place's unique personality can it become a remarkable and competitive place. Tell your community's story and build upon it.

My contribution to this long conversation on character and uniqueness of places is this—a simple restatement of everything that too many leaders, thinkers, and professionals in our field can't yet grasp:

There can't be a formula for any of this.

At the beginning, I stated that there are few new ideas in this book. If you're seeking easy solutions there are libraries full of ideas. But if you're genuinely concerned for the future of our places I hope that you stop looking for them and instead inhabit The Local.

Now put down this book and go start making your community stand out as remarkable in the world. Spark your design genius. And always remember that how places become local starts with you; You're The Local.

It's finally time for all of us to start designing for you.

ABOUT ME

I'm Kyle Ezell, AICP, and I'm an Associate Professor of Practice of City and Regional Planning at The Ohio State University's Knowlton School and the recipient of numerous teaching awards including the College of Engineering's Distinguished Faculty Award for Outstanding Teaching and Ohio State University's Excellence in Community-Based Scholarship. I am also a principal of a planning, design, and public participation firm called Designing Local, Ltd. where I attempt to live up to the values and expectations I set forth in this book.

See what I'm up to by visiting

WWW.DESIGNINGLOCAL.COM

YOUR WORK

If you are designing local in your community, please share your work with me at Hi@designinglocal.com.

CPSIA information can be obtained at www.ICGtesting.com
Printed in the USA
LVOW04s2353051114

412271LV00014B/294/P

9 780692 233306